GOD

+

MUSIC

=

JOY

"...but those who hope in the LORD will renew their strength. They will soar on wings like eagles; they will run and not grow weary, they will walk and not be faint."

Isaiah 40:31

Endurance + Hope + Faith=
REward + JOY= (REJOICE!)

When asked, "What brings you the most joy?", the most popular optimistic answers among group members were God/higher power and music. I refer to Bible verses that reinforce various elements and misunderstandings about joy. Furthermore, I selected various songs that correspond to each reinforcement depicted; Listen to them during your free time! The last page of this book contains the playlist of all songs mentioned.

Joy is a manifestation and sensation, not a destination. Joy and happiness are benevolent outcomes from optimistic and simple daily living. It is not a destination associated with obtaining and accomplishing what individuals perceive as a means of eternal happiness.

Such accomplishments include mundane and paramount factors such as wealth, career success, true love, new friendships, soul renewal in a spiritual establishment, a clean house, or arrival of benevolent mail.

The danger of placing an emphasis on a scenario is low gratitude for present blessings and high spirits of greed. It is human nature to strive for more. However, when excessive, an individual will be more vulnerable to burn out. It breeds a spirit of tireless ambition and accomplishment.

In addition, joy occurs due to factors within your control as opposed to factors outside of your control. For example, joy is more abundant when controllable development of self-love as opposed to an uncontrollable factor of joy such as finding true love and true friendship.

James 1:2-3

My brethren, **count it all joy** when you fall in various trials, knowing that the testing of your faith produces patience

Try listening to "Mad" by Solange and Lil Wayne as a soothing tune to channel the energy of anger! Anger over past trauma, present injustices, and future uncertainties is just. However, it is not worth your precious spirit fruit of joy to be consumed by the unfairness of life.

The past cannot be changed. The future is not a promise. The present moment must be driven by a motivation to retain joy. Joy is not all bubble gum and rainbows. Joy and anger cannot coexist as anger rots the fruit of Joy.

Count your blessings! Do not take your series of negative life events to heart. No matter how life seems unfortunate, always count your blessings! There is a large design and plan behind every positive, negative, and indifferent series of events within your life span development.

Cherish the positive. Learn from the negative. Take indifferent experiences into positive coping skill utilization. Spiritual, mental, emotional, and physical health is a top priority!

Psalm 47:1

Clap your hands, all your nations; shout to God with cries of joy.

Listen to "Happy" by Pharrell Williams. Take steps to be joyful! There are activities that start with letters A through Z (Acting, Bowling, Billiards, Belly Dancing through ZUMBA® are just a few).

Ladies, pamper yourself through simultaneous stimulation of the mind, body, heart, and soul! Fellas, have recreation and leisure fun when you need a masculine escape. Breathe fresh air for vitality. Step out of your comfort zone to make the most of your life.

Labor of love comes in many forms. My Joy is obtained while I read and write about Nutrition, Health, and Self Improvement. Productivity and joy go hand in hand. Idle time is the predominant time of distraction and joylessness. Wisdom is a guide and by-product of labor that is based on your unique life purpose that God called for you to do.

Your life purpose on Earth will make Earth as close to Heaven as possible in your own right. Fame and fortune are not a necessity to make a mark in the world. I find more joy as a Nutrition Counselor and Nutrition Writer than I ever could as a public figure or celebrity.

Life is not always a picnic but you can cultivate your own picnic basket to your own accord! Have a picnic on your own lawn, beach, or park with your family, friends, and romantic partner instead of going out to eat. Make sandwiches, pack healthy snacks, and have fun! Learn from the ants rather than stomp on them.

Proverbs 6:6-8

"Go to the ant, O sluggard; consider her ways, and be wise. Without having any chief, officer, or ruler, she prepares her bread in summer and gathers her food in harvest."

Ants are not the biggest animals or the loudest. They are the most diligent and wise. Ants store and gather food in hills. Ants work together in unison. Once you channel your inner ant, you are more likely to draw in others with an optimistic and benevolent inner ant.

The body of Christ will then have a strong structure and function. A body of Christ that reflects God's love for you is evident when you have the family members, love match, friendships, community, and/or occupation that He designed just for YOU!

Isaiah 9:3

You have enlarged the nation and increased their joy;

they rejoice before you as people rejoice at the harvest, as **warriors** rejoice when dividing the plunder.

Listen to the song "Warrior Song" by Nas and Alicia Keys. It cheers and pumps me up! Triumph, joy, and enthusiasm manifests and inspires others to obtain and increase spirits of joy.

Spread joy by being a positive person to be around. It all starts in the mind! People will be drawn to you once you exude a positive aura and energy. Benevolent forces will enhance your joyful energy.

There will be those that may test you and challenge you but stay strong! Change your way of thinking about these individuals. Individuals cannot be changed without their own accountability and desire to change. They can only be accepted as they are. Laugh off those who make you feel weaker than you are. Do not take them personally.

Your test develops into your victory and testimony! Believe, have faith, and know that everything happens for a reason. You have the choice to channel your inner warrior or inner victim. Your individual triumph spreads to your loved ones and community members.

Change your thoughts and perceptions. Deviant behavior has

an origin of negative thoughts, feelings, attitudes, perceptions, and beliefs. Negative thoughts manifest negative feelings, followed by negative attitudes, beliefs, actions, and decisions. Every manifestation whether positive, negative, or indifferent starts in the mind. Change your thoughts into truth of triumph and it manifests in glorious aftermath!

Ecclesiastes 9:7

"Go, eat your food with gladness, and drink your wine with a joyful heart, for God has already approved what you do."

Eating disorders (anorexia nervosa, bulimia nervosa, and overeating) are dangerous, fatal, and unnecessary. Your body is a temple and a gift- no matter what shade or size! Consume adequate and balanced nutrition (whole grains, lean protein/dairy, fish & plant-based oils, and a rainbow of fruits & veggies) with occasional treats such as dark chocolate! Start small with dietary changes. Try one brand new fruit and one new vegetable per grocery trip!

The song "Smile" by musician Vitamin C has refreshing dance rhythms with splashes of reggae through legendary musician Lady Saw. Have oranges as a snack while listening to her entire upbeat self-titled album!

Dance and strut in your favorite swimwear to simulate a Caribbean getaway! It's a mini vacay right at home without spending frivolously! Listen to the album "Caribbean Party Music"! It has a wonderful mix of tropical instrumental music.

Heart ache, sorrow, depression, anxiety, doubt, panic, rejection, and other pessimistic emotions are not combatted with excessive eating, drinking alcohol, and using substances. Although wine consumption is encouraged in the Bible, it is not a necessity to feel merry.

Alcohol and drugs are a temporary solution. Once the inebriation wears off, there is physical, mental, spiritual, and emotional weariness, distress, and pain. Emotional eating is also common. There are individuals that eat more when happy, more when sad, less when happy, and less when sad. See Romans 14:17.

Healthier habits combat shortcomings that are held at an unrealistic standard. As a Nutrition Counselor and Writer, my advice in this book concerning nutrition, health, wellness, and recreation have authentic and genuine information.

2 John 1:12

I have much to write to you, but I do not want to use paper and ink.

Instead, I hope to visit you and talk with you face to face, so that our joy may be complete.

The written and spoken word is powerful. Words can heal or hurt people. "Beautiful" by Christina Aguilera is a song that reinforces beliefs she and her listeners must have about their own beauty, regardless of unkind words.

In a sharp and dark contrast, words can hurt people as well. It is amplified in a digitally socialized world with cases of cyber bullying affecting all individuals of human categorization. Negative blogs and gossip are financially rewarded in the world. Try your best to not get caught up in it!

2 John 1:12 reinforces how encouraging written exchanges are a component and not an entirety of complete joy. Live socialization, social skill development, interview skill development, and unity complete the package.

Socialization and intimacy are scarce in today's world. Social media is the prime basis of contemporary connections and communication. It is common to attend a social gathering with individuals plugged into technology devices.

Social media addiction is unfortunately authentic and was

depicted in an episode of MTV's "True Life". The basis of social media addiction is insecurity. A state of euphoria emulates a "high" and is reached when a status, tweet, or selfie is liked, shared, retweeted, or complimented.

There are individuals that have a lot to say through a computer screen but lack necessary life skills such as oral communication, public speaking, building natural rapport with a romantic interest, and interview skills.

Social media perception makes individuals feel inadequate, unattractive, lonely, depressed, and unlovable when taken too seriously. Wedding pictures sadden single, divorced, and widowed men and women. Baby pictures sadden the childless. Travel pictures sadden those who do not have the time, money, circumstances, or resources to travel.

Pictures associated with career success diminishes the spirit of those who are not where they want to be with their career. Family and friendship pictures sadden the friendless and those without a family support system. Pictures of "perfect" and "flawless" models and celebrities with a popular following amplifies low self-esteem among impressionable individuals.

Social media is an illusion. People present the best versions of themselves through pictures and words. Images are digitally enhanced with computer software programs. Beauty products for hair, skin, makeup, and nails, are sold through manipulation and propaganda.

Hair length and volume is glamorized through shampoo commercials regardless how all textures and lengths of hair have strength and beauty. Makeup commercials reinvent aesthetic trends and standards to retain relevancy and innovation. Nail length is an illusion and will not be obtained through the purchase of unnatural beauty products.

The beauty industry defies acceptance of innate features associated with each heritage. Spirituality of all forms, when optimistically used, promotes how there is a loving plan and purpose behind the soul, heart, mind, and body of everyone. Everyone is blessed regardless of life circumstances, social status, heritage, physical appearance, relationship status, fashion sense, and other methods to promote division of humanity.

Joy is manifested through contagiously optimistic socialization. There are studies that prove how isolated individuals have a shorter life span and negative quality of life than those who socialize more. Suicide rates are higher in rural and desolate regions of the United States.

Substance use and abuse etiology, in college settings particularly, is linked to sociological reasons such as "to decrease social anxiety, to have the courage to talk to a crush/potential mates, to "have something to do" in a "boring" college and location, peer pressure, to have fun/party, and to provide an escape from loneliness and stress."

There are enhanced consequences in conventionally nocturnal settings under the influence of alcohol and drugs such as physical assault, domestic violence, dating violence, sexual assault, rage, aggression, fueled arguments that lead to broken relationships and friendships, self-mutilation, gun violence, memory loss, loss of assets, incarceration, decreased academic and employment performance, expulsion, automobile accidents, suicide, and vehicular homicide. However, marketing associated with alcoholic beverages overtly and subliminally promotes and glamorizes socialization and intimacy in negative social settings.

Positive socialization with a recreational and sentimental theme promotes health, wellness, connection, and fun without placing freedom, health, livelihood, and life span in jeopardy. Recreational substances are unnecessary to have a good time.

Nehemiah 10:10

The joy of the Lord is your strength!

Joy (an optimistic state associated with Spiritual, Mental, Emotional, and Physical Health) and Strength (Spiritual, Mental, Emotional, and Physical) go hand in hand. There is a mind-body connection.

Provide proper fuel for yourself to stimulate all areas of your health. Participate in physical activity that you personally enjoy rather than what is "trendy" and unnecessarily expensive.

Interests evolve- go with rather than against your own personal grain. A nostalgic, fierce, and fun reminder of joyous strength is "Stronger" by Britney Spears. Listen to it for an instant boost!

Isaiah 35:10

"…and those the LORD has
rescued will return.

They will enter Zion with
singing; everlasting joy will crown
their heads.

Gladness and joy will overtake
them, and sorrow and sighing will
flee away."

Listen to the song "To Zion" by
timeless and powerful lyricist
Lauryn Hill and soothing and epic
guitarra de Carlos Santana. Their
musical marks are iconic!

Esther 8:17

In every province and in every city to which the edict of the king came, there was joy and gladness among the Jews, with feasting and celebrating. And many people of other nationalities became Jews because fear of the Jews had seized them.

The Bible perceives Judaism believers as unforgivable enemies. The Holocaust was pernicious, tragic, and unnecessary. Listen to "Beatbox" by Jewish reggae and hip-hop artist Matisyahu.

Enhance *joie de vivre* in positive ways to stay out of trouble. Take nature walks/jogs, dance, lift weights, play basketball, pray/meditate, read, write, draw, color, and practice yoga. Individuals are happier when participating in active rather than passive activities. Develop a hobby, skill, creative craft, anything! Use finances to buy inexpensive books to learn a new language or skill. The possibilities are endless when used wisely.

Psalm 27:6

Then my head will be exalted above the enemies who surround me;

at his sacred tent I will sacrifice with shouts of joy;

I will sing and make music to the LORD.

Listen to "Shake It Off" by Taylor Swift. Don't worry about what your enemies say or think. Enroll in classes and workshops to step out of your comfort zone and have fun! Visual and performing arts classes and workshops serve as excellent vessels to enhance creativity, imagination, self-expression, and overall quality of life.

It does not matter if it is at the *American Idol, X Factor, Grammy, Emmy, Tony Award, Ted Talk, Def Comedy Jam, New York Times,* and *Academy Award* status. Sing, write, act, dance, orate, paint, photograph, tell jokes, film, and make music from your heart.

Invest into music, art, drama, or dance therapy or just go for it! Music therapists provide psychological perspectives through the beautiful art of music. Songwriting structure and intrinsic wellness are simultaneously enhanced and reinforced. Music therapy turns the mute and inarticulate into voices with power and boldness. Watch "King of Speech" as an inspirational movie to find your voice.

It is not necessary to always be a soprano and the center of attention. It is unnecessary to thrive in a "selfie" digital age at the expense of building true social, romantic, and professional connections.

The background has less chaos, increased peace, and immense JOY! Kudos are great as a sign of appreciation and affirmation. However, there is less pressure to live up to unnecessary standards for females and males alike.

The media is dishonest with images about what to look like. Plastic surgery, diet pills, and anabolic substances are unnecessary and fatal. It puts money in their pocket when told what standards to live up to. Be yourself and thrive!

Proverbs 15:23

"A man has joy in an apt answer,
and how delightful is a timely
word!"

It is draining and
unnecessary to have something to
say 24/7. There does not always
have to be a victorious champion in
a debate, argument, or
disagreement. There are those
whose views are parallel to yours.
There are contrasting perspectives
that you can learn from. There are
those whose views of the world
may never change. You do not
have to go out of your way to prove
yourself.

It is pointless to have the last
word and impossible to have every
answer. Delight arises temporarily

with a smart aleck comment. Contemporary communication amplifies the rush of sharing a viral opinion rather than a quotidian fact. However, true joy comes from silence and taking your time to speak.

Listen to "Megalomaniac" by Incubus to rock out against all the narcissists and motor mouths. There are "know-it-alls" and opinionated people everywhere in the world. We all have a unique perspective and view of the world. Never conform your views due to an "intimidating" megalomaniac. There are those who think they are better than everyone else. Do not lose sleep about what others think, say, or do about you, the world, or anything that you have going on.

Their opinion does not matter. Listen to "It Doesn't Matter" by Wyclef Jean and Dwayne "The Rock" Johnson whenever you get caught up in the materialism, narcissism, and pessimism of other people.

Think before you speak. There are consequences when an unkind word is spoken such as the loss of intrinsic and extrinsic respect, loss of friendships, loss of intimate partners, broken family ties, loss of jobs, loss of freedom when violently manifested, and even loss of lives through suicide or homicide.

Psalm 30:5

"Weeping may endure for a night,
but joy comes in the morning."

There are many benefits to be
a morning person. It is essential for
your soul, heart, mind, and body to
begin the day and set the tone on a
positive note. Start your day by
blasting "A Brand New Day
(Live)" by The Wiz Cast. Every
day is a new slate. Relax, thrive,
and evolve!

Night-time could be a sad
time, especially when single or in
an unhappy relationship.
Nocturnal settings heighten
negative escape mechanisms. I
personally spend nights dancing at
home, singing karaoke, doing
yoga, cleaning, making

collages/scrapbooking, writing, reading, and doing independent research.

Do what makes you happy based on personal preference. It is ideal to be "square", quirky, fun, and "weird" than a detrimental, destructive, and dangerous party animal. Nights should be utilized in positive ways to combat sadness and loneliness that amplifies at night-time.

Do not fret over your relationship status. Use your singlehood to discover yourself, and therefore, attract people that enhance your strengths and improve your weaknesses. Do not stay in a relationship or friendship clique to appear established, popular, or happy. Popularity is not a component for happiness.

People must lift you up and be conducive to your ascension as a human being. It is more important for people in your own life to respect and accept you due to authenticity. It is unnecessary to be deemed relevant and cool by peers due to a misrepresentation or facade. Conformity diminishes the spirit of joy.

Be your own lover! Buy dark chocolate and strawberries for Valentine's Day for yourself. Watch a movie in cute and inexpensive Loungewear. Do not fret over name brand items. Anyone who judges where you shop, nitpicks your personal fashion style, and assesses your status based on what you are wearing is not worth your time.

Romans 15:13

"May the God of hope fill you with all joy and peace as you trust in Him, so that you may overflow with hope by the power of the Holy Spirit."

We are human and perfectionism is a dangerous and unrealistic goal. Joy is obtained when the need to control, change, and ponder over people, places, things, ideas, and experiences of the past, present, and future is released. Joy comes from a peaceful perception and acceptance of good, bad, and indifferent past experiences with a positive, hopeful, and triumphant outlook on the present and future.

Everything truly happens for a reason. Trust is a necessary component to obtain joy. Trust and have hope that things will work out for you and that all events in your life are working for rather than against you. Everything comes full circle to contribute to your life span development. Let it Be! Listen to "Let it Be" by the Beatles to peacefully remind you! Another song to refresh your outlook on how things are manifesting for your benefit is "I'm Better" by Missy Elliot and LAMB.

Matthew 6:25-26

"I tell you, do not be anxious about your life, what you will eat or what you will drink, nor about your body, what you will put on. Is not life more than food, and the body more than clothing? Look at the birds of the air: they neither sow nor reap, nor gather into barns, and yet your Heavenly Father feeds them. Are you not of more value than they?"

Fashion is fun but try your best to keep it in moderation. Shopping is an amazing method to celebrate accomplishments such as weight loss. Have pride in your own personal style. It is not coined cool just because a mainstream fashion show, fashion magazine editor, fashion critic, fashion designer, celebrity, or model is wearing it or talking about it. If you do like designer and name-brand fashion, check out consignment boutiques and thrift shops.

Reggae legends Bob Marley and Bobby McFerrin have excellent tracks that correspond to Matthew 6:25-26. Listen to "Three Little Birds" by Bob Marley and "Don't Worry Be Happy" by Bobby McFerrin to exude a [No Worries] demeanor.

Anxiety diminishes after joy is amplified. Peace and Love are enhanced through these soothing reggae tracks. I believe that it is no coincidence that Peace and Love sandwich Joy as listed fruits of the Spirit in Galatians 5.

God + Music = Joy Playlist

"Mad" by Solange and Lil Wayne
"Happy" by Pharrell Williams
"Warrior Song" by Nas and Alicia Keys
"Smile" by Vitamin C and Lady Saw
"Beautiful" by Christina Aguilera
"Stronger" by Britney Spears
"To Zion" by Lauryn Hill and Carlos Santana
"Beatbox" by Matisyahu
"Shake it Off" by Taylor Swift
"Megalomaniac" by Incubus
"It Doesn't Matter" by Wyclef Jean and Dwayne Johnson
" A Brand New Day (Live)" by "The Wiz" Cast
"Let it Be" by the Beatles
"I'm Better" by Missy Elliott and LAMB
"Don't Worry Be Happy" by Bobby McFerrin
"Three Little Birds" by Bob Marley

www.ingramcontent.com/pod-product-compliance
Lightning Source LLC
Chambersburg PA
CBHW071747020426
42331CB00008B/2204